MW00988342

NO-TILL
GARDENING

THE ORGANIC METHOD FOR RICHER SOIL, HEALTHIER CROPS, AND FEWER WEEDS

Caleb Warnock

THE BACKYARD RENAISSANCE COLLECTION

DISCOVER THE
LONG-LOST SKILLS OF
SELF-RELIANCE

y name is Caleb Warnock, and I've been working for years to learn how to return to forgotten skills, the skills of our ancestors. As our world becomes increasingly unstable, self-reliance becomes invaluable. Throughout this series, *The Backyard Renaissance*, I will share with you the lost skills of self-sufficiency and healthy living. Come with me and other do-it-yourself experimenters, and rediscover the joy and success of simple self-reliance.

FAMILIUS

Copyright © 2015 by Caleb Warnock

Published by Familius LLC, www.familius.com

Familius books are available at special discounts for bulk purchases for sales promotions or for family or corporate use. Special editions, including personalized covers, excerpts of existing books, or books with corporate logos, can be created in large quantities for special needs. For more information, contact Premium Sales at 559-876-2170 or email specialmarkets@familius.com.

Library of Congress Cataloging-in-Publication Data
2015957942   ISBN 9781942934080

Edited by Amy Stewart
Cover design by David Miles
Book design by David Miles and Brooke Jorden
Photography by Caleb Warnock and Wikimedia Commons

10 9 8 7 6 5 4 3 2 1
First Edition

CONTENTS

FiFTEEN REASONS TO NEVER TiLL YOUR GARDEN AGAiN!

NO-TILL GARDENING:

1 Dramatically reduces the work required to garden

2 Reduces weeding by 90 percent

3 Allows you to establish a self-seeding garden

4 Means you never need to purchase fertilizer again

5 Hugely cuts down on soil disease

6 Cuts down on soil compaction

7 Dramatically increases natural soil fertility

8   Makes a 100-percent organic garden practical

9   Makes gardening physically accessible

10 Makes permaculture truly possible—no gas, no tiller

11 Makes a garden honestly sustainable

12 Makes gardening easier for beginners, experienced growers, the physically disabled, seniors, children, and families

13 Increases yields

14 Makes a larger garden possible with less work

15 Makes gardening less expensive

WELCOME TO A BETTER, SIMPLER GARDEN

There are only two ways to make soil fertile. One way is natural; the other way is synthetic. The natural way costs nothing and requires little work. The synthetic method is expensive and labor intensive, and it violates the first rule of sustainable gardening: the garden should pay you—you shouldn't pay the garden by buying stuff for it.

You may be surprised to learn that the natural method is based almost solely on mushrooms. Mother Nature has a whole system of soil fertility in place, and as it turns out, if we get out of her way, she will make our gardens fertile—for free.

Modern science has confirmed something surprising. In natural ecosystems, many if not all plants are best able to remove nutrients from soil with the help of mushroom mycelium. Most gardeners have never heard of mycelium, even though they've seen it. The mushroom is an interesting plant. The entire plant is underground. Only the fruit—what we call "mushrooms"—emerges into the sunlight. The rest of the plant is called *mycelium* (in plural form, *mycelia*). If you've ever turned over an old log or cleaned a garden in spring, you've likely seen the brilliant white threads that are mycelium. These strings are delicate and easily destroyed, but when left to their own devices, they will slowly break down the largest logs, straw, chaff, and garden waste, helping Mother Nature turn these things into rich soil.

Mushroom mycelium growing on wood in the author's garden.

Mushrooms are huge plants, with the mycelium of one plant running for dozens, hundreds, or thousands of feet under the soil. Mushroom plants thread themselves through the soil where they assist trees, bushes, grasses, and vegetables. The roots of all the plants that surround us need the help of mycelium to get food from the soil. It's that simple.

When we mechanically till the soil, we are damaging the very mycelium that our soil relies on for natural health. Until the modern age, gardening was always done using the no-till method, and this book will show just how easy it is to return to our roots (pun intended).

THE MYSTERY OF ROOTS

In school, we teach children that if you plant a seed, it sprouts in soil and grows. This is almost the whole knowledge of most adults too, even if they are avid gardeners. We put seeds into the ground, and we hope they sprout and grow.

This rudimentary understanding leaves out some important questions:

- What is soil made of?
- Where do the nutrients in the soil come from?
- How do plants take nutrients from the soil?

The reason these questions are rarely discussed is that, believe it or not, we don't really know the answers. The more we study soil, the more complex it turns out to be.

The quest to understand how soil works began by accident.

In about 1880, a man named A. B. Frank, living in Prussia, was commissioned by "His Excellency, the Minister of Agriculture, Domains and Forestry"[1] to figure out how Prussia could start cultivating truffles—those delicious and expensive mushrooms. While studying truffles, Frank stumbled upon a major scientific breakthrough.

What was known by mushroom experts in the 1880s was that truffles grew only around the roots of three kinds of trees—beeches, oaks, and a tree that Frank called "hornbeam." Frank began using a microscope to examine the soil and tree roots. In 1885, when Frank published a groundbreaking paper, the newest microscope technology allowed him to magnify objects up to six hundred times their size. Imagine Frank's surprise when he turned a microscope onto the tips of the roots of the trees where truffles grew and found something "not heretofore even slightly suspected by science," as he put it. "Certain tree species . . . do not nourish themselves independently in the soil but regularly establish a symbiosis with fungal mycelium over their entire root system. This mycelium performs a 'wet nurse' function and performs the entire nourishment of the tree from the soil."[2]

What Frank's microscope allowed him to see, for the first time in the history of the world, was that the rootlets were completely enclosed by a "mantle of fungal hyphae . . . forming a continuous cover even over the growing tip." Frank coined this new discovery "mycorrhiza," based on a Greek word (in Greek, *mycos* means "fungus" and *riza* means "roots").[3]

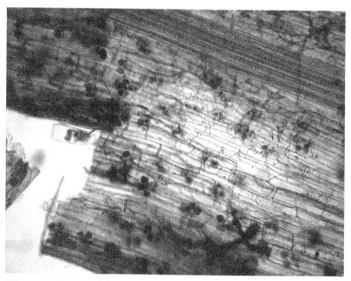

Microscopic view of fungal hyphae among plant root cells.

Today, science has shown that "mycorrhizal symbiosis is the most ancient, widespread form of fungal symbiosis with plants" and "plants formed associations with . . . fungi . . . about 460 million years ago. . . . This is estimated to be some 300 to 400 million years before the appearance of root nodule symbioses with nitrogen-fixing bacteria."[4]

Though we have known for 130 years that plants depend on mycelium, we know very little about the whole process. We know that, for the most part, mushroom plants must have carbon to live but that they are not able to process this carbon themselves. To solve this problem, they form relationships with plants underground. The plants provide carbon to the mushrooms, and the mushrooms "farm" these plants by supplying them with nutrients so the plants will continue to grow and provide carbon.

In 2008, the Oxford *Journal of Experimental Botany* published a wide-ranging paper[5] that examined years of studies of mycelium and its relationship to plants. Here is what modern science has learned about this relationship:

- Mycorrhizal fungi "connect" plants to the "nutrients required for their growth."
- Mycelium helps plants in times of stress, including drought, soil acidification, and exposure to toxic metals and plant pathogens.
- Mycelia increase "the nutrient absorptive surface area of their host plant root systems."

- "Fungi play a central role" in "influencing soil fertility, decomposition, cycling of minerals and organic matter, as well as plant health and nutrition."

- At least 250,000 kinds of plants use something called "arbuscular mycorrhizal" mushroom mycelium to get nutrients from the soil, and scientists believe the number is actually much higher.

- In areas with poor soil, *Ericoid mycorrhiza* grows with about 3,400 species of dwarf shrubs. One species, *Rhizoscyphus ericae*, "penetrates the cell walls of roots and forms coiled structures within each cell."

- Many trees and perennial plants depend on ectomycorrhiza; ten thousand fungal species and eight thousand plant species may be involved globally. "Although this represents only a small fraction of the total number of terrestrial plants, these species often form the dominant components of forest ecosystems occupying a disproportionately large area. . . . The fungi do not penetrate the host cells, and the symbiosis is characterized by the presence of a fungal mantle or sheath around each of the short roots."

- "Extraradical mycelium may form a significant fraction of the total microbial biomass in forest soils."

- Most of the time, the mushroom plants depend on their

host plants for essential carbon, but in some cases, the roles are reversed. About four hundred plant species have dust-like seeds that "are initially entirely dependent upon the supply of carbon and nitrogen from fungi. . . . The fungi colonizing these plants were originally thought to be effective saprotrophs or parasites, but DNA-based studies of the fungi have now shown that most of them are mycorrhizal fungi simultaneously colonizing other autotrophic plants."

- Mycelium is made up of individual microscopic threads called *hyphae*, which are "able to penetrate soil microsites which are inaccessible to plant roots."

- "Mycorrhizal mycelia, either by themselves or in association with bacteria or other fungi, may actively release nutrients from mineral particles and rock surfaces through weathering" by producing natural acids.

- In 1997, evidence was published showing that some granite rock is "commonly criss-crossed" by microscopic networks of tubular pores which might be caused by "fungi exuding organic acids at their tips." This means that fungi might literally be slowly "eating" rocks to provide nutrients for plants, but this theory is still debated and more study is needed.

- High-tech X-rays have shown that certain mushroom

plants "eat" minerals called *apatite* and *biotite* to "mobilize significant amounts" of phosphorus and potassium and "probably [play] a significant role in transporting these to trees."

- Lichens weather ("eat") rocks by producing organic acids.
- "Mycorrhizal fungi may play a significant role" in taking nitrogen and phosphorus from large molecules in nature called *polymers*, "which are otherwise unavailable to plant roots."
- Mycorrhizal fungi take nitrogen and phosphorus from other sources, such as pollen, dead nematodes, and other kinds of mycelia, and make them available to plants.
- Different kinds of fungi dominate different layers of soil. Saprotrophic fungi dominate newly fallen leaf litter on the forest floor (anything that has fallen within the past four years). In the more decomposed layer underneath that, mycorrhizal fungi are dominant, and they take up nitrogen and make it available to their host plants.
- Certain fungi create a "rapid" flow of carbon through the soil.
- There is evidence that mushroom plants may decompose certain kinds of soil pollution, including pesticides and plastics, but it is unclear whether the mushroom plants

are just moving the pollution or if they are rendering it harmless. However, all efforts to transplant fungi into contaminated areas for natural healing have failed because fungi is notoriously hard to transplant. There is also evidence that certain bacterias known to help heal soil pollution thrive better when grown with mycelium.

- Mycorrhizal fungi help plants fight off "metal toxicity, oxidative stress, water stress, and effects of soil acidification." Very little is known about how this works, especially regarding metal toxicity.

- Experiments have shown that the more diversity of fungi there is belowground, the more diversity of plants there is aboveground in natural grasslands. The relationship is not fully understood.

- A three-way symbiotic relationship between bacteria, plants, and fungi appears to provide nitrogen to plants in some circumstances.

Thanks to modern science, our old understanding of soil is giving way to a new understanding. The plants that cover our world today "do so because selection has favoured different types of symbiotic association" with mycorrhizal fungi to distribute nutrients, "enabling the flow of energy-rich compounds required for nutrient mobilization."

NOTES

1. A. B. Frank, "On the nutritional dependence of certain trees on root symbiosis with belowground fungi," trans. James M. Trappe, *Mycorrhiza* 15 (2005): 267, http://www.researchgate.net/profile/James_Trappe/publication/8178699_On_the_nutritional_dependence_of_certain_trees_on_root_symbiosis_with_below-ground_fungi_(an_English_translation_of_A.B._Frank's_classic_paper_of_1885)/links/004635216ff5a1f36d000000.pdf.

2. Ibid.

3. Ibid.

4. Roger D. Finlay, "Ecological aspects of mycorrhizal symbiosis: with special emphasis on the functional diversity of interactions involving the extraradical mycelium," *Journal of Experimental Botany* 59, no. 5 (2008): 1115. http://jxb.oxfordjournals.org/content/59/5/1115.full.pdf

5. Ibid, 1115–1123.

A HISTORY OF GARDEN TILLING

Mechanical tilling is, of course, a modern invention. Throughout history, gardening has been done using the no-till method.

Perhaps the oldest written references to garden tilling are found—you guessed it—in the Bible. In the second chapter of Genesis, we read that the Garden of Eden sat unused because "there was not a man to till the ground,"[1] so God himself "planted a garden eastward in Eden."[2] In the next chapter, we read that Adam and Eve were kicked out of Eden "to till the ground"[3] for food.

Today, "tilling" means mixing soil, but for most of the history of the world, tilling meant something entirely different: turning the soil. Shovels, plows, and hoes have been used for centuries to turn the soil. For the most part, this was simply a way to get clear ground. Weeds were removed by turning them upside down and burying them underneath the ground. The weeds became fertile compost as they began to decompose. The cleared land left by turning could be made into a garden, allowing the gardener to plant seeds. Weeds would sprout too, but the seeds planted by the garden had a better chance of outcompeting the weeds.

Enter the mechanical tilling machine.

The garden tiller was invented in Australia by Arthur Clifford Howard and patented in 1920. It was called a "rotary hoe." Howard originally envisioned it as a tool for gardeners, but gardeners rejected his work, not wanting to purchase it because it was not necessary. Howard created a larger model for farms and began to see success, although the growth of his company was stymied by World War I and then by the Great Depression. Fun fact: Howard eventually trademarked his invention as the "Rotavator," which is one of the longest palindromes of the English language.

The whole problem with rototillers is summed up in the name given to these machines in Germany. Arthur Howard eventually made agreements with companies in Germany and elsewhere to manufacture his tillers for Europe because it was too expensive to export them from Australia. The German company Siemens, which was among the first to import tillers to the United States, called them *boden fräsen*, which means "earth grinder."

Earth grinders, indeed.

The machine that gardeners had initially rejected was soon popular among farmers worldwide because it allowed them to clear huge tracts of land faster. Howard began to invent tractors to pull his tillers, and both the tractors and tillers got larger and larger. Small family farms began to give way to huge industrial "power farms."

The problem was that tilling drastically reduced soil fertility because it did so much damage to the soil. What kind of damage? The mechanical action not only destroyed the mycelium but also ground the earth so finely that it created compaction. And tilled topsoil, essentially ground into dust, continues to this day to blow away, creating huge fertility problems worldwide. Science solved these problems by creating commercial, petroleum-based fertilizers that could be scattered over fields and mixed right into the soil with Howard's new tiller machines. Natural soil fertility was no longer necessary.

Problem solved. The new science of agronomy promised to end starvation forever.

Soon, superfertilizers were being produced. My grandfather, who worked for decades for Ortho Laboratories as a chemist, was among the vanguard in this work. His name was listed on many Ortho patents for fertilizers and other agricultural chemicals. It was an exciting time for science. My grandfather and his fellow scientists were literally making food bigger. Chemical fertilizers could produce huge ears of corn and help industrial farms triple their yield. Following the horrors of World War I, twenty million people starved to death in World War II. People like my grandfather vowed this would never happen again. America became the breadbasket of the world.

As petrochemicals became the standard on farms, backyard gardeners began to "see the light." Arthur Howard's invention had initially been rejected by gardeners as useless, but soon the wave of science washed over the backyard garden too. Organic gardening methods were dropped, seen as old-fashioned and foolish.

The great age of chemicals had dawned.

NOTES

1. Genesis 2:5 (AKJV).
2. Genesis 2:8 (AKJV).
3. Genesis 3:23 (AKJV).

A HiSTORY Of NO-DiG GARDENING

I n 1937, Masanobu Fukuoka, a twenty-five-year-old microbiologist, became desperately ill with pneumonia. As has happened with so many people, myself included, nearly dying changed him. While hospitalized, he had a revelation about who he wanted to be. "In an instant, I had become a different person," he wrote. "I sensed that, with the clearing of the dawn mist, I had been transformed completely, body and soul."[1]

After getting his health back, Fukuoka quit his job as an agricultural inspector and returned to his family's farm of orange groves. For the next fifty years, he taught the world about the dangers of modern farming.

Because modern food production "is based upon the flawed concepts of Western philosophy, which put man in conflict with his environment, we now selfishly exploit and destroy nature for our own ends," Fukuoka said in a 1988 speech while accepting the Ramon Magsaysay Award for

Public Service. "Agriculture has degenerated into an industrial and commercial process driven by human desires, making us slaves to money and to oil. . . . Based on the conviction that genuine truth, beauty, and pleasure can be found only in nature, I have pursued a 'do-nothing,' natural way of farming—with no tilling, no fertilizer, and no chemicals."[2]

At this point, we should stop to ask a hard question:

ARE YOU AND I SLAVES TO OIL?

To answer this question, you must know where fertilizer comes from. Almost all modern food that is for sale, whether in a grocery store or a restaurant, is grown using fertilizer. In the United States, the vast majority of this fertilizer comes from the island nation of Trinidad and Tobago, where it is made from natural gas in pollution-belching factories.

Read that twice—that fertilizer that you put on your lawn and garden is made from natural gas, and almost 60 percent of it in the United States is imported from Trinidad and Tobago. The next biggest supplier is Ukraine. It has been decades since the United States self-reliantly produced fertilizer. Take a moment to let that sink in. Our food supply depends on other countries.

No oil (natural gas)? No food!

Japan, which is one of the world's largest consumers of

agricultural chemicals per capita, did not listen to Fukuoka when he wrote his book, but he found a surprise audience in Europe and America, where there was growing dissatisfaction with corporate reliance and the dearth of natural food. Published in English in 1978, *The One-Straw Revolution* has been called the taproot for the worldwide permaculture movement. Because of this book, many people have changed the way they eat.

Interestingly, *Fukuoka* means "hill of good fortune" in Japanese. *Permaculture* is a word that means "to live and eat in a way that is permanent." Nature is permanent and self-sustaining. The idea is that living in a way that destroys what is natural cannot last. After all, the natural world is all we have. Everything unnatural that we create—plastics, chemicals, synthetic fertilizers, superfoods, power farming—depends on nature for its basic ingredients. Power farming has fed millions, but if it destroys nature, it destroys the whole system—humans, too.

NOTES

1. Masanobu Fukuoka, *The Ultimatum of GOD NATURE: The One-Straw Revolution, A Recapitulation*, trans. Shou Shin Sha, (Oohira, Ehimeken, Japan: 1996): 2, https://seedzen.files.wordpress.com/2012/03/fukuoka-masanobu-the-ultimatum-of-god-nature-the-one-straw-revolution-a-recapitulation-1996.pdf.

2. "Fukuoka, Masanobu," Ramon Magsaysay Award Foundation, http://www.rmaf.org.ph/newrmaf/main/awardees/awardee/profile/292.

CALEB'S HiSTORY WiTH NO-DiG GARDENiNG

hen I was a boy growing up on our family farm, I spent the summers working in our fields, where we raised corn, barley, wheat, and alfalfa. Both my father and my grandfather warned me sternly that when the airplane flew over to drop pesticide and herbicide on our land, I should run to make sure I was not hit with the spray. Or, if I could not outrun the airplane, I should hold my breath as long as possible to avoid breathing in the chemical mist as it settled around me. Summer after summer, I would watch as the airplane zipped back and forth, leaving behind its weed- and bug-killing fog.

When I was a young man, my father drove me across the railroad tracks into our cornfield, where we carefully measured the height of our cornstalks and the length of the gleaming yellow ears. My father was participating in a contest, sponsored by the county agriculture department, to see which farmer could grow the tallest corn and get the fields with the greatest yield per acre. I was tall for my age, but the corn towered over me, shooting up toward the sky. I remember my father proudly pronouncing one crop to be the tallest we had ever grown.

This was the world I knew. My grandfather was an Ortho chemist. My other grandfather owned one of the largest farms in the county. My father and I prided ourselves on the height of our petrochemical-fueled corn. In our tiny rural town, the surest sign of prosperity was a brand-new monster tractor glittering in the harsh desert sun—something my father never owned. I remember feeling concerned that I would be poisoned by the tractors pulling sprayers and the airplanes spreading fog, but I didn't question the necessity of any of it. It was simply the way farming was done.

While I eventually did leave the farm for college, I never left gardening. In my book *More Forgotten Skills*[1] is a picture of me in my garden—on land borrowed from elderly neighbors—on the day I graduated from college. I stood by my tomatoes in my graduation gown. Penniless, I could not afford a tiller and I did all the work with a shovel, and even the shovel threatened to break my meager bank account. But I loved the taste of fresh food, and I loved to have my hands in the soil. I scattered the white crystals from the bag of store-bought fertilizer, just as my grandparents and parents had done, hoeing the fertilizer into the rows before planting my seeds. Paying for a bag of fertilizer was a sacrifice at a time when I had nothing, but I thought that without it, my garden would be a laughingstock. That is what I had been told by experts. I had heard of organic gardening, but the experts scoffed, calling it a fool's errand. God had given the world petrochemical fertilizer as a mark of this generation's greatness, as a sign of man's power and dominion over the elements.

But all around me, a counterculture was growing. My parents had a subscription to a groundbreaking magazine called *Mother Earth News*, which in those days was tantamount to having the word *HIPPIE* tattooed on your forehead. I pored over those magazines, baffled that people would try to build houses out of straw bales. The magazine was part of my father's self-reliance period, during which he made horrible stinky cheese—dyed orange—on our kitchen table while my mother churned butter from the milk of our cows. My parents tried to garden. We got a few summer squash and tomatoes, but their foray into hippiedom didn't last. Eventually, my mother went back to teaching and my father tried to cash in—successfully, at first—on the real estate craze. Meanwhile, our small farm plodded on, until my grandfather, the only one in the family who owned a tractor, sold his farm and died.

So much for the counterculture.

I was an odd amalgam of my parents and grandparents. After a day at the newspaper office, I would come home and make jam from our backyard grapes and raspberries. The first purchase my wife and I ever made together was a garden tiller. (I transplanted her raspberries on our first date.) I made homemade bread, and we grew a bountiful garden. I began to ask questions—how did homesteaders of yore make bread without store-bought yeast? That question eventually lead to my coauthored book, *The Art of Baking with Natural Yeast*[2], which has been called "groundbreaking." How did my ancestors feed their chickens without going to the farm supply store for chicken feed? How did the world feed itself in winter before the grocery store? That question led to my bestselling *Backyard Winter Gardening*[3] book. My hippie wife and I slowly became more and more self-reliant, loving the freedom and the taste of our homegrown food. Our garden expanded and expanded.

One afternoon, after hours of tilling, I turned off the machine and sat down for a minute to take in the beautiful sight of a perfectly clean garden—not a weed in sight, the dark soil freshly turned, practically begging for seeds and water. Every year, I took a picture of this moment because I knew from hard experience it was a sight I would not see again for a full year—a garden free of weeds. Within forty-eight hours of being watered, my clean tilth would be marred with weeds. I would spend the summer on my hands and knees, fighting the weeds. But on this day, my stepdaughter, Mysti, wandered out of the house to admire my work. Offhand, she remarked that one day she wanted to have a no-till garden.

A what?

I had never heard the term before. She had read something, she said, about a new method of gardening without tilling.

"What would be the point of that?" I questioned.

"It makes the soil better," she said.

From that moment fourteen years ago to this day, I have never tilled my garden again. Eventually, we gave our tiller away.

I have always loved to learn. In my childhood home, learning—especially from books—was the highest virtue. From that day, when I first heard the words "no-till gardening," I began to research. I couldn't find a single person who had ever tried it (this was before the invention of Facebook with its multitude of local, national, and international gardening groups). But I began to read about how tilling destroys garden fertility and forces gardeners to use chemical fertilizers. I had thought the garden methods I grew up with were simply "the way it's done," but I learned that since World War II, we have been producing vegetables in ways that have never been tried before in the history of the world. While tilling and chemical fertilizers do what they claim to do, there are natural consequences that cannot be escaped. And increasingly, these consequences cannot be ignored.

The first of these consequences is that we have been working far, *far* harder in our gardens than we need to—stupidly hard, ridiculously, pathetically hard. The second is the famous "$64 tomato."

In 2006, author William Alexander released *The $64 Tomato*[4], his scorching critique of all gardening. The subtitle says it all: *How One Man Nearly Lost His Sanity, Spent a Fortune, and Endured an Existential Crisis in the Quest for the Perfect Garden*. His book is a mocking memoir of how stupid backyard gardening has become. Alexander took the amount he had spent on building and maintaining his garden, amortized it over twenty years, and subtracted what it would have cost him to buy at a farm stand the food he had grown. The result? His tomatoes had cost him a staggering

$64 *each*. I remember thinking, as I read the *New York Times* review of his book, that he must be a staggering moron to have spent that much money trying to get a Martha Stewart–esque garden. He argues that beautiful, bountiful gardens are a thing of another age—an age when people had either slaves or servants.

Horsepucky.

The $64 tomato is a modern invention—an invention of global conglomerates that need us to buy fertilizer, pesticide, herbicide, hybrid vegetable and flower seed, soil additives, white vinyl garden boxes, mycorrhizal fungi granules, imported beneficial insects, soil acidifier, pre-emergents, weed barrier, garden decor, and, of course, a tiller. I clearly remember the day I saw a segment on television in which the famed Martha Stewart had hired a crew to remove all the native soil in her garden down six astonishing feet and replace it with premium soil she had brought in by the semitruckload . I was gobsmacked. I remember thinking, *Is that how wealthy people garden? I should give up! Maybe only the obscenely rich can have gardens worthy of magazine spreads.*

I was right. Or wrong, depending on what kind of magazine you turn to for inspiration.

After a tour of my backyard, a blogger once wrote this about my garden: "It's not beautiful, but it is productive." I've never forgotten the shock—I think my garden is one of the world's most beautiful places. Truly and genuinely, that is how I feel. It took me a long time to process this blogger's underhanded scolding, calling my garden "not beautiful." So you can imagine my delight when I read how the Ramon Magsaysay Award Foundation described Masanobu Fukuoka's world-renowned garden in Japan: "His untidy farm." I *love* it!

> His untidy farm yields grain and fruits just as abun-
> dantly as high-technology farms, often more so, and
> a rich mix of hearty vegetables besides. His method
> offers farmers extra leisure. It requires no expensive
> inputs. It creates no pollution. Moreover, it is profit-
> able. . . . He does not plow his fields, nor weed them
> by tillage or herbicides. He does not plant seeds in
> tidy rows but casts them randomly upon the ground.
> He uses no machines, no insecticides, and no chem-
> ical fertilizers or prepared compost; he strews his
> rice and barley fields with straw instead," wrote the
> Magsaysay Foundation. And what does no-till gar-
> dening replace? The modern way of "disturbing the
> self-balancing processes of nature . . . creating weak,
> chemical-dependent plants and poisoning the land,
> water, and air.[5]

"When you get right down to it, there are few agricultural practices that are really necessary," said Fukuoka.[6]

Recently, there was a group of people touring my garden after one of my classes. One of the women stopped in the middle of my onion bed and exclaimed, "I can't wait to go home and tell my husband that you are eating all these weeds I have been pulling up for years!"

I still do some weeding, but far, far less than I used to do. We encourage wild edibles in our garden, eating the purslane and making homemade cheese with the mallow.

I hope this book on no-till gardening will be as much of a revelation—and a relief—to you as this method has been for me. Prepare yourself for a new world of backyard gardening that is much cheaper, far simpler, and easier on the conscience.

NOTES

1. Caleb Warnock, *More Forgotten Skills of Self-Sufficiency* (Springville, UT: Cedar Fort, Inc., 2014).

2. Caleb Warnock and Melissa Richardson, *The Art of Baking with Natural Yeast: Breads, Pancakes, Waffles, Cinnamon Rolls & Muffins* (Springville, UT: Cedar Fort, Inc., 2012).

3. Caleb Warnock, *Backyard Winter Gardening: Vegetables Fresh and Simple, in Any Climate, without Artificial Heat or Electricity—the Way It's Been Done for 2,000 Years* (Springville, UT: Cedar Fort, Inc., 2013).

4. William Alexander, *The $64 Tomato: How One Man Nearly Lost His Sanity, Spent a Fortune, and Endured an Existential Crisis in the Quest for the Perfect Garden* (Chapel Hill, NC: Algonquin Books, 2006).

5. "Fukuoka, Masanobu," Ramon Magsaysay Award Foundation, http://www.rmaf.org.ph/newrmaf/main/awardees/awardee/profile/292.

6. Ibid.

//

NATURAL MYCOSYSTEMS: MUSHROOMS HEAL GARDENS

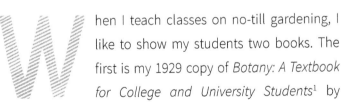 hen I teach classes on no-till gardening, I like to show my students two books. The first is my 1929 copy of *Botany: A Textbook for College and University Students*[1] by William Robbins and Harold Rickett. The second is my 2005 copy of *Mycelium Running: How Mushrooms Can Help Save*

the World by the renowned and beloved Paul Stamets. The contrast between these two books is stark. While the knowledge of mycelium in 1929 was enormous compared to 1880, it seems crude in comparison to Paul Stamets's 2005 book. And yet, as Stamets points out, what we now know is just a drop in a mysterious ocean. The more we learn, the more we realize that we don't know much.

What we do know is this: different kinds of mycelia do different jobs in nature. Some break big things down. Some break small things down. Some transport nutrients.

According to Stamets[2]:

- Experiments show that mycelium may be sentient. It can choose the shortest path to food.

- Mycelium produces natural chemicals, called *enzymes*, and acids to break down natural materials.

- Mycelium is either primary, secondary, or tertiary, meaning that some perform a primary function in nature and the others help afterward. For example, a primary mycelium breaks down fallen trees and dead plants. A secondary mycelium then comes in to break down what the primary creates. A tertiary then breaks down what the secondary creates into basic nutrients like nitrogen and phosphorus. (By the way, this natural archetype is also true of colors. Red, yellow, and blue are primary colors;

orange, green, and purple are secondary colors (created from the primary colors); and all other colors are tertiary to these.)

- There are seven known types of mycelium, defined by the broad jobs they do in nature.
- Mycelium forms "mats" in the soil, often near the surface but sometimes deeper. These mats have been documented in forests at thousands of acres in size and thousands of years old. We are just beginning to understand this relatively new science. According to BBC Earth, the world's largest living organism is believed to be a honey fungus in Oregon.[3]
- Ants and other insects cultivate or farm specific mycelia, which produce antibiotics for parasites that kill ants.
- Shaded baby trees in the forest—with no light—are fed sugar by mycelia. Without mushroom plants, these baby trees would die. The same mycelium has been documented to provide three different foods to three different trees.

When it comes to no-till gardening, there are three kinds of mycelium that we are trying to protect in our soil:

1. *Ectomycorrhizae* is a family of mycelia that sheath plant roots to protect and feed them.

2   *Endomycorrhizae* is a family of mycelia that live inside plant roots, protecting and feeding them.

3   *Endophytes* are a family of mycelia that thread around (but not through) cell walls within roots and stave off infection, parasites, insects, drought, and heat.

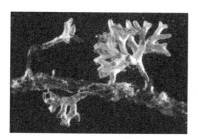 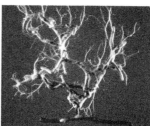

Microscopic view of ectomycorrhizae (left) and endomycorrhizae (right)

The importance of these mycelia on the farm and in the garden cannot be overstated. According to Stamets[2]:

- Tests show wheat grows 30 percent larger when paired with certain endophytes.

- Seed germination goes from 57 percent to 95 percent when paired with certain endophytes.

- A plant's root mass doubles when paired with certain endophytes.

- "Clearly, pairing . . . endophytes with agricultural crops can increase yield, decrease disease, and reduce the need for fertilizers and insecticides."

- Experiments have shown that pairing grass and wheat with certain endophytes can greatly increase their tolerance to drought and heat. Exactly how this works is not understood.

- Tests have shown that leftovers from "poofed" mushrooms (those that have released their spores and died) heal mortally wounded trees.

Mushrooms in the author's garden

- Mycelium exhales carbon dioxide, which is heavier than air and settles in the soil and then is taken up by plant roots. Plants "eat" carbon dioxide and exhale oxygen.

- "Mycelium moves nutrients, including rare earth elements, over distances to give to plants."
- Tests and pictures show a huge difference between gardening with spores and with no spores.
- "All gardeners are mushroom growers already—most just don't know it."
- Today, many gardeners are mushroom killers. We till just when the mycelium is beginning to run the strongest.
- Mycelium is hard to "transplant." The most expensive mushroom in the world is the perigord truffle, and people have spent millions of dollars over decades trying to farm them with no luck. They have never been grown in a laboratory successfully.

We cannot just throw mycorrhizal spores into our gardens, even though they are sold widely for that purpose. That is a short-term benefit at best. Mycelium must colonize naturally for sustained growth.

This means no tilling.

Spores are airborne and are everywhere. They love raised beds. Why? They love untreated wood. They perform best when not walked on repeatedly. Mycelium runs through weed fabric, which is not a solid sheet but a fabric with holes.

Just before this book went to press, new mushroom

research generated global headlines like these: "Mushrooms make it rain"[4] and "Mushrooms promote downpours."[5]

New research published in the venerated scientific journal PLOS ONE on Oct. 28, 2015 said that, for the first time, scientists had documented mushrooms appearing to influence the weather. "Mushrooms as rainmakers: How spores act as nuclei for raindrops" was the title of the research, done at Miami University. Researchers said, "millions of tons of fungal spores are dispersed in the atmosphere every year. These living cells, along with plant spores and pollen grains, may act as nuclei for condensation of water in clouds."

Using an electron microscope, scientists discovered that water condenses onto the airborne spores. The researchers concluded:

> The kinetics of this process suggest that basidiospores are especially effective as nuclei for the formation of large water drops in clouds. Through this mechanism, mushroom spores may promote rainfall in ecosystems that support large populations of ectomycorrhizal and saprotrophic basidiomycetes. Our research heightens interest in the global significance of the fungi and raises additional concerns about the sustainability of forests that depend on heavy precipitation.[6]

NOTES

1. William J. Robbins and Harold W. Rickett, *Botany: A Textbook for College and University Students* (New York: D. Van Nostrand Company, Inc., 1929).

2. Paul Stamets, *Mycelium Running: How Mushrooms Can Help Save the World* (Berkeley, CA: Ten Speed Press, 2005).

3. Nic Fleming, "The Largest Living Thing on Earth Is a Humongous Fungus," BBC Earth, November 19, 2014, http://www.bbc.com/earth/story/20141114-the-biggest-organism-in-the-world.

4. Maribeth O. Hassett, Mark W. F. Fischer, and Nicholas P. Money, "Mushrooms as Rainmakers: How Spores Act as Nuclei for Raindrops," PLOS One, http://journals.plos.org/plosone/article?id=10.1371/journal.pone.0140407

5. Michael Harthorne, "Mushrooms Make It Rain," Newser, http://www.newser.com/story/215247/mushrooms-make-it-rain.html

6. Jennifer Viegas, "Mushrooms Promote Downpours," Discovery News, http://news.discovery.com/earth/mushrooms-promote-downpours-151028.htm#mkcpgn=rssnws1

A portion of a "fairy circle" or "elf circle" of fruiting mushrooms

FOUR METHODS OF NO-TILL GARDENING

THE OLD-FASHIONED METHOD

B y "old-fashioned," I mean *ancient*. Any plot of land that you garden without tilling is a "no-till garden," but you need to control the weeds to make your garden a happier, more successful place. For at least two thousand years, if not more, the way people controlled weeds was by using natural compost.

Animal manure was put into piles or into raised beds. (For a history of raised-bed gardening, see *More Forgotten Skills*.[1]) This manure naturally became hot as it began to decompose. The heat was highest at the center of the pile. A skilled composter could make piles that got hot enough to kill the weed seeds inside the manure. In this way, layers of weed-free compost were created, allowing for no-till garden-ing with little interference from weeds.

You can still practice this method today if you are up to the challenge, but my experience shows me that while our ancestors relied on manure in the garden, today people would rather stop gardening forever than deal with trying to gather and compost animal manure. I include this method in case you really want a "natural" garden—but most people don't want to be that natural! Here are three other methods that most modern gardeners find more helpful:

THE OPEN-GROUND METHOD

 Spread weed fabric (also called *landscape fabric* or *weed barrier*, available at home improvement stores and garden centers) over the ground in your garden. We do this to control the weeds. Get professional-quality, thick weed fabric that is guar-anteed to last at least a decade. At this writing, a 100-foot roll of professional-grade weed fabric costs me about $70. If you don't want to control the weeds, then you don't need to do any of the steps in this method. You can just stop tilling your garden, and you will have a no-till garden. However, in my experience, weeds are the biggest reason people give up gardening. Controlling the weeds means that you are more likely to be a happy gardener for many years to come. If you have horrible rhizomatous weeds, like crabgrass, you will likely need three layers of weed fabric. Crabgrass will grow right through a single layer.

2 Cut a few holes in the fabric. I suggest a hole the size of your hand every 5 feet, but you don't have to be precise. This gives access to worms, which spread mycelium spores and are important to soil health. The holes also give your no-till garden access to connect to the larger mycosystem. However, if you have crabgrass, don't cut holes—the long rhizome roots will travel more than twenty feet under weed fabric to infest the hole!

3 Cover the weed fabric with a thin layer—1–2 inches—of untreated wood chips. Mycelia love to "eat" wood chips, and this guarantees that mycelia will quickly "run" in your new garden.

4 Cover the wood chips with a layer of compost as deep as you want. I suggest organic, weed-free compost. (Compost, available at home improvement stores, is made weed-free by natural heating that kills weed seeds.) For most vegetables, 2 or 3 inches of compost or even less will be perfect. Carrots, parsnips, and potatoes will need deeper compost.

5 Put down stepping stones. The goal is to avoid compacting the earth where you will be growing, so put down stepping stones to create a walking path. The rest of the garden should not be walked on if possible.

Stepping stones forming a pathway in one of the author's gardens

6   Plant in and water your garden as you like. The mycelium will naturally come to colonize your new soil. How? Woodchips naturally have mycelium spores on them. Water has spores in it. Wind has spores. Rain is filled with spores, as is snow. Wherever you live, there are lots of natural mycelium spores waiting to find a new home. Once you have created your no-till garden, the spores will automatically do their job, and the soil will grow better and more fertile as the years go by without tilling.

THE RAISED-BED METHOD

Gardening in raised beds offers some advantages over gardening on open ground. Raised beds allow you to control weeds, improve the soil, and define paths so you can avoid compacting the planting beds by walking on them.

1   Spread weed fabric (also called *landscape fabric* or *weed barrier*, available at home improvement stores and garden centers) over the ground in your garden. We do this to control the weeds. Get professional-quality, thick weed fabric that is guaranteed to last at least a decade. If you have horrible rhizomatous

weeds, like crabgrass, you will likely need three layers of weed fabric.

2   Build a raised-bed frame from untreated lumber.
This can be as simple or elaborate as you wish. If you
live in a dry climate, like I do, use screws and 2x4 or
2x6 lumber to make a bed about 8 feet long and 3
feet wide. In dry climates, you want your bed as low
as possible so you don't have to water so much and
so the roots of your plants have access to the native
soil below the weed fabric. The roots will go down
through the weed fabric. If you live in a place with
humidity and rain, you may want to make all your
beds 12 inches tall. If your bed is too long, it will bow
out in the center over time. If it is too wide, you won't
be able to reach into the center of it, and the center
will not only be wasted space but will also become
weedy over time. For detailed advice about raised
beds, see *More Forgotten Skills*.[2]

3   Cut a hole the size of your hand in the weed fabric
at the center of the raised bed. This gives access to
worms, which spread mycelium spores and are important to soil health. The hole also gives your no-till
garden access to connect to the larger mycosystem.

4 Fill the raised bed half full of wood chips or shredded wood. Use only untreated wood. Mycelia love to "eat" wood chips, and this guarantees that mycelia will quickly "run" in your new garden. (Carrots, parsnips and potatoes will need a deeper raised bed with no wood chips at all.)

5 Fill the rest of the raised bed with compost. I suggest organic, weed-free compost. The level of compost will sink over time, so I suggest you overfill the raised bed so that your compost is at least 1 inch above the top of the bed. Once you start watering and planting, the compost will flatten out and compact some.

6 Plant and water your garden as you like. The mycelium will naturally come to colonize your new soil. How? Wood naturally has mycelium spores on it. Water has spores in it. Wind has spores. Rain is filled with spores, as is snow. Wherever you live, there are lots of natural mycelium spores waiting to find a new home. Once you have created your no-till garden, the spores will automatically do their job, and the soil will grow better and more fertile as the years go by without tilling.

One of the author's raised-bed gardens

HUGELKULTUR

In general, the word *hugelkultur* in gardening means "hill culture." First, you make a pile of logs. Then you top it with branches. You top the branches with leaves, and the leaves with soil or compost. The point of this is to create a mound that absorbs the natural rains so you can garden without ever watering. The problem is that hugelkultur, as you may have guessed from the name, is a concept that was created in Germany in the 1970s. I have been to Germany, and I can tell you from experience that it is a beautiful, lush, green country where it rains. Where I live, it does not rain. Where I live, if you created a mound like this, the water would simply drain away. So if you live in a lush, rainy place, the traditional hugelkultur concept is for you.

If you live in a desert, like I do, hugelkultur is best done in an enclosed space. I use huge metal livestock troughs, which I purchase used from farmers looking to get rid of them, usually for about $20 apiece. I fill at least the bottom half with wood, packed as tight as I can get it. This wood is trimmings from our orchard. In the spring, I have huge mushrooms in my metal hugelkultur, which come bursting out of the soil from the wood under the compost.

1 Decide if you are living in a humid climate or a dry climate. For a humid, wet climate, build a traditional hugelkultur mound as described above. You can learn more about this by Googling "hugelkultur." Or you can use a livestock trough with drain holes or a large raised bed. If you live in a dry climate, find something large without drain holes, like a livestock watering trough.

2 Add wood. How much wood you add depends on what you want to do with the hugelkultur. No matter where you live, you need to fill your hugelkultur at least half full with packed wood. If you live in a dry area, use more wood. If you intend to grow carrots, parsnips, or potatoes in your hugelkultur, you will need at least twelve inches of compost at the top of the wood. Almost everything else can be grown in four to five inches of compost, and "surface" crops like lettuces and greens will need even less. If you live in a dry area, the less compost you have, the less you will need to water. True hugelkultur shouldn't be watered ever, but if you are growing lettuce in twelve inches of compost, meaning that your lettuce is twelve inches away from the wood that absorbs

and traps the natural rain and snowmelt, then you are going to have a problem. In a dry area, the roots of your plants need to be as close to the wood in the hugelkultur as possible, because the wood is where the water is stored.

3 Top with compost. How deep should your compost be? See Step 2.

QUESTIONS AND ANSWERS ABOUT THE FOUR NO-TILL METHODS

Q: Can you use paper in place of weed fabric?

A: You can use a paper liner—the thicker the better—to stop weeds. Several inches is best. Over time, however, the paper will decompose and weeds may creep in, especially if you have rhizomatous weeds like crabgrass.

Q: Can I use cardboard as my liner?

A: No. Cardboard is made with glue, which is made of chemicals you may not want in your garden.

Q: *Back to Eden*[3] says I should just lay down a bunch of wood chips. Isn't this easier than your method?

A: I have never seen the film *Back to Eden*, but I know lots of people who have put down wood chips "because *Back to Eden* told me to." Their gardens have been fairly free of weeds but infested with bugs that damage their vegetables. This is the reason we don't just put a whole bunch of wood chips on the ground—the bugs will move in and their population will explode. Pillbugs in particular (also called "potato bugs" or "roly polies") love this environment, and they will ravenously eat holes in your root vegetables and attack the stems of your other vegetables, doing a lot of damage if their numbers are uncontrolled. Covering the ground with weed fabric first keeps the bug population from exploding because there is not moist housing under the wood chips—just weed fabric. Wood chips, by the way, are not natural—there were no wood chips in Eden. Wood chips are made with petroleum-fueled machines. Weed fabric (a fine plastic mesh) is also a petroleum product, so either way you are using a petroleum product, but one method creates uncontrolled insect problems and the other, using weed fabric, does not. If you want a no-till garden without plastic, use the Old-Fashioned Method.

Q: Does compost contain mycelium spores?

A: No. Mycelium spores are generally killed at 120 degrees, while weed seeds must be heated at 140 degrees for a length of time to be killed. (Compost is naturally, not mechanically, heated, though most manufacturers mechanically pump air into the compost pile to speed the process). Compost can naturally heat up to 150 degrees or more, so the mycelium spores are killed in the process. But this does not matter, because mycelium spores in innumerable amounts surround us all the time, just waiting for the right conditions to sprout in the soil. We need our compost to be free of viable weed seeds, so it needs to be heated, but the compost will quickly be colonized by the natural mycelium spores found in water, air, and snow and naturally spread by worms.

NOTES

1. Caleb Warnock, *More Forgotten Skills of Self-Sufficiency* (Springville, UT: Cedar Fort, Inc., 2014).

2. Ibid.

3. *Back to Eden*, directed and produced by Dana Richardson and Sarah Zentz (Big Sur, CA: Dana and Sarah Films, 2011), DVD.

CREATING A SELF-SEEDING NO-TILL GARDEN

elf-seeding is only possible in no-till gardens. *Self-seeding* means that the vegetables plant themselves naturally without me lifting a finger except to provide water in the summer. (I live in the high desert in Utah, and I watered my garden four times last year.) How does self-seeding work? Like this:

- I plant natural, nonhybrid, heirloom, open-pollinated seeds (this is what I sell at SeedRenaissance. com). The plants grow. I harvest what I need, reserving at least ten plants, which I allow to go to seed. I keep the seed from naturally crossing using isolation. The seeds fall to the earth at the end of the season. In the autumn or spring, they germinate on their own. I do absolutely nothing. I don't rake them; I don't plant them; I don't do a single thing to help them. As it turns out, Mother

Nature knows what she is doing without my help, as long as I don't get in her way by tilling or using hybrid or GMO seeds!

- From then on, I reserve at least ten plants each year to go to seed. I "reserve" them by simply not eating them. Each year, the plants go to seed and grow themselves the next year. I do nothing. It's the best gardening method ever invented, and guess who invented it? Mother Nature.

Let me give you an example. I once planted Snow Fairy tomatoes in my garden. Some of the tomatoes fell to the ground during the season. I didn't clean them up. The next summer, the tomatoes sprouted in the garden on their own. Since then, they have sprouted each year. They produce ripe tomatoes faster than the tomatoes I start months earlier in my greenhouse. My self-seeding tomatoes don't even sprout until July, but once they sprout, they grow like a wildfire, while the transplanted tomatoes sit in shock, trying to get used to their new life. This is just one example of many.

For a list of self-seeding vegetables, look under the self-seeding category at SeedRenaissance.com. Seeds must be heirloom and tested for this trait. Not all heirlooms readily self-seed. Hybrid and GMO seeds are self-suiciding. You can read much more about this in my books *Forgotten Skills*[1] and *More Forgotten Skills*[2]. My garden in spring, autumn, and winter is 80 percent self-seeding (meaning that I plant only 20 percent of what I harvest). In the summer, my garden is about 60 percent self-seeding.

NOTES

1. Caleb Warnock, *The Forgotten Skills of Self-Sufficiency Used by the Mormon Pioneers* (Springville, UT: Cedar Fort, Inc., 2011).

2. Caleb Warnock, *More Forgotten Skills of Self-Sufficiency* (Springville, UT: Cedar Fort, Inc., 2014).

One of the author's gardens in early summer

NEVER PURCHASE FERTILIZER AGAIN!

CALEB'S RECIPES FOR FREE HOMEMADE FERTILIZER

ost natural vegetables don't need fertilizer in a no-till garden. There are three exceptions that need a dose of homemade fertilizer once a month. They are:

1 Corn

2 Potatoes

3 Mangels (Almost no one grows mangels anymore. Mangels are huge beets—thirty pounds each—that were grown for centuries as the food that kept livestock alive through the winter.)

Here are two recipes for fertilizer you can make yourself:

COMPOST FERTILIZER TEA

Step 1: Fill any size of bucket one-third full with compost. This should be finished compost, meaning that no matter what it started out as, it has now all turned into rich black soil (or brown, in the case of mushroom compost). It should be cool to the touch, not hot. Hot compost is still breaking down. This compost can be of your own making or purchased.

Raised beds waiting to be planted in the author's spring garden

2 Step 2: Fill the rest of the bucket with water. Leave this outside to sit in a sunny place for three sunny days. You are essentially making sun tea out of compost. If you don't have three sunny days in a row, wait until you have a total of three sunny days or one week of other days, whichever comes first.

3 Step 3: Stir the compost tea, preferably with something disposable, like a stick. Get two more buckets that are roughly the same size as the one you are using for the tea. Pour one-third of the tea into each bucket. You now have three filled buckets, each one-third full with the ripe tea.

4 Step 4: Fill each of the buckets with water. This step is essential. Compost tea that is not diluted can be too "hot," which means it is too rich in nutrients and can damage your plants. By filling your buckets with water, you have diluted the tea using a two-to-one ratio—one part compost tea, two parts water.

5 Step 5: Use the diluted tea to water your garden. You can pour it into a garden watering can, or you can do what I do—take the bucket and pour it over the plants. Just be careful not to get the tea on yourself, because it will stain clothes and shoes and it does have an odor.

GREEN LEAF FERTILIZER TEA

Because compost is usually in short supply in my garden (because I use so much of it), I use this recipe most often. The upside is that you don't have to use your homemade or purchased compost. The downside is that this recipe has a stronger odor than compost tea. If you have a small property with close neighbors who might be offended by a little stinkiness for a couple of days, this might not be the recipe for you. You can use the compost tea recipe.

 Step 1: Fill any size of bucket one-third full of green leaves of any kind. These can be weeds from the garden, the outer leaves of vegetable plants (like the outer lettuce leaves you would probably not use anyway), vegetables (leaves and bulbs) that have been munched on by chickens, or a rabbit, or a caterpillar, or grasshoppers (What's that, you say—this only happens in my garden?!), leaves from trees (fresh, not dried), chemical-free grass clippings, or anything green. If you are using weeds, do not include weeds

that have seeds on them. Weeds in flower are fine. The roots are fine. Dirt on the roots is fine. You can use all the same kind of leaves or a mixture of any kind of leaves. You can break open the baseball bat zucchinis and add them in or tomatoes that were touching the ground and have begun to rot—anything from the garden that is vegetative and alive.

Step 2: Fill the rest of the bucket with water. Leave this outside to sit in a sunny place for three sunny days. You are essentially making sun tea out of green leaves. If you don't have three sunny days in a row, wait until you have a total of three sunny days or one week of other days, whichever comes first.

Step 3: When the tea is ripe, carefully pour the water out of the bucket into another bucket, leaving behind the spent greens. The spent greens, which have now discolored, can be buried in the compost pit or compost pile (or hot bed). If you don't bury them, they will smell for several days.

Step 4: Stir the leaf tea, preferably with something disposable, like a stick. Get two more buckets that are roughly the same size as the one you are using for the tea. Pour one-third of the tea into each bucket. You now have three filled buckets, each one-third full with the ripe tea.

Step 5: Fill each of the buckets with water. This step is essential. Leaf tea that is not diluted can be too "hot," which means it is too rich in nutrients and can damage your plants. By filling your buckets with water, you have diluted the tea using a two-to-one ratio—one part compost tea, two parts water. This makes it safe for your plants.

Step 6: Use the diluted tea to water your garden. You can pour it into a garden watering can, or you can do what I do—take the bucket and pour it over the plants. Just be careful not to get the tea on yourself, because it will stain clothes and shoes and it does have a strong odor. Don't worry; the odor disappears in a day or two—but not from the bucket. Rinse out the bucket with a hose, preferably over lawn grass, which can benefit from the residual nutrients.

QUESTIONS AND ANSWERS ABOUT HOMEMADE FERTILIZER

Q: How much is a "dose" of this homemade fertilizer?

A: Enough to really soak the soil—as much as you would water if you were watering the garden with a watering can. There is no need for a precise measurement. You are simply giving the plants a good drink.

Q: Can I use my lawn grass clippings?

A: Up to you. Did you put chemicals on your lawn grass? If yes, do you want those chemicals in your garden? I don't think so.

Q: Can I spray the tea on as foliar fertilizer (fertilizer sprayed on the leaves of the plant to be absorbed through the leaves)?

A: Yes, if you spray it by itself. If you put it into a garden hose attachment, it's going to be too diluted. (Remember, you already diluted it once.) And if you try to put it in undiluted, it will stink and it won't be diluted to the right ratio. Why bother, anyway? What is the point of using it as foliar spray? It's easier and faster to just water your plants with it.

Q: How soon after I use the fertilizer can I eat my vegetables?

A: Wash them, then eat them.

Q: How soon do I need to use the tea?

A: It can sit for several weeks if you like. It might develop a harmless white mold on the top, which you can skim off with a stick and throw out. The smell will get stronger. Your neighbors might glare at you. Don't let the kids or the dog accidently tip it over onto them—they will stink to high heaven, even after you wash them with soap.

Q: Can I bottle it up to save for later?

A: Must you? Well, if you must, then yes, you can. However, only store the diluted tea—never store the undiluted tea, because it might develop gases and explode out of your container. Never store in the sun or heat for that same reason. Your best bet is just to not store it, or if you want to store it, don't store it for very long, or in any place where you will mind terribly if it leaks or explodes and stinks. Don't store it in glass jars, because of that whole explosion thing I just mentioned. Don't blame me if it explodes or leaks. And don't complain to me, either. You're on your own, baby!

Q: Can I put a lid on the bucket in case it smells or cover the bucket in some other way?

A: No, especially not if you are making the Green Leaf Fertilizer Tea. A closed container is very likely to explode, kind of like making homemade root beer that is allowed to ferment, and thus carbonate, too much. You might be able to cover the bucket to make compost tea, but I have never tried it with a lid, so you will be experimenting.

A carrot from the author's greenhouse with mycelium on the root

USING NO-TILL GARDENING FOR ALL-NATURAL DISEASE CONTROL

I n healthy soil, beneficial bacteria outcompete harmful bacteria with the help of mycelium enzymes and acids. If this were not true, the earth would be wiped out by the dangerous "bad" bacteria and viruses that surround us all the time. Every living thing on the planet has everything needed to decompose it on its surface, just waiting—including us. If that were not true, the earth would be covered in a deep layer of dead bodies. The same thing is true of every plant and animal. Mother Nature has a whole plan that allows bacteria and viruses to do their job when needed. The "good" bacteria keep the bad stuff naturally in check and do not let it grow out of control. Because of this, the no-till garden is naturally disease and pest resistant. The less we do, the healthier the garden is.

QUESTIONS AND ANSWERS ABOUT NO-TILL GARDENING

Q: How does the no-till method reduce the work required to garden?

A: You don't need to turn the garden with a shovel, you don't need to rattle your bones with a tiller, you don't need to spend much time weeding, and if you plant self-seeding varieties, you don't need to spend much time planting, either. All you have to do is harvest and relax. I know it sounds too good to be true. I don't know how else to convince you except to say "Try it." You can look for video tours of my garden on YouTube (http://bit.ly/1M60CMl) if you want to see my garden "in action."

Q: How does no-till gardening reduce weeding by 90 percent?

A: Each of the no-till methods I've outlined in this book is based on controlling weeds. Garden beds, as well as pathways between raised beds, can be covered with weed fabric to make life easier. To get rid of weeds, we simply design our garden with weed control in mind.

Q: How does the no-till method make gardening more physically accessible?

A: Several ways. First, you don't have to till! Second, weeding is dramatically reduced. Third, raised beds can be tall enough for gardening at your comfort level. Fourth, you can create hugelkultur container beds, with drain holes in moist climates and without in dry climates, that make gardening possible at the perfect height for you. I severely injured myself a couple of years ago, tearing the muscle and tendon away from my pelvic bone in four places. This injury has never healed, and I am now in the midst of a series of three surgical procedures in addition to a second round of physical therapy. (Ironically, I injured myself doing a reverse butterfly in yoga class.) In the past two years, I have become much more appreciative of the need for the garden to be accessible to everyone, despite age or ability. Even people in wheelchairs can garden when the garden is custom designed.

Q: How does the no-till method make true permaculture gardening possible?

A: For starters, there is no ongoing need for gasoline or a mechanical tiller. There is no need for machinery or petroleum of any kind.

I acknowledge that all plastic is a petroleum-derived product, so our garden hoses, some garden gloves, and the underground pipes that bring water to our gardens are all plastic. Even weed fabric is plastic. We can't escape plastic and, thus, our reliance on petroleum. But we can get rid of our direct need for gasoline and machines in the garden.

True permaculture means that we eat from and manage our land with very little impact to our property—without chemicals, synthetic fertilizers, and purchased "inputs" that modern gardens seem to die without. Permaculture is the belief that natural methods are valuable and important. Forty and fifty years ago, the national motto seemed to be "Better living with chemistry." Today, we know from hard experience that chemicals are just as dangerous as they are helpful. The real problem is this: chemicals are easy to use and give quick results, but the consequences last generations.

In the canyon next to my home, miners took out gold, silver, and copper more than one hundred years ago. To get the valuable metals out of the ore, they used chemicals like arsenic and heavy metals. In those days, their eyes were on the prize of money. They dumped the waste chemicals straight into the ground. To this day, you can still see exactly where they performed this work because the land is stained and discolored (yellow), and nothing—not a single thing—grows on the poisoned land. The miners got a few bucks, and more than a century later, the creeks that run near the slag piles are too poisonous for fish and cannot be used for drinking water.

Those miners literally poisoned the earth for generations to come. Did they stop to think about this? Did they care? Did they know what they were doing? I have no idea. But today, we have no excuse. We know exactly what the long-term ramifications of chemicals are. We know our synthetic fertilizer is running through the groundwater and into the ocean, causing algae blooms that are killing the native fish. You can read about fertilizer pollution easily by typing "fertilizer algae" into Google News. We know that pesticides are killing children—even in my county, children have died when people hired companies to spray their home for spiders! We know that we have created air pollution and that our children have asthma (and, according to new research, perhaps autism) because of it. We know we have polluted the water and that fish die in droves—birds too—and some water is too dangerous to drink (do a little research online to find out how the manufacturing of cell phones and computers is poisoning whole cities and water supplies in third-world countries). We know what we are doing to the land, water, and air is making people sick. We know it doesn't work. We have not yet, at least not as a whole society, decided that we must change. Why? Because change requires sacrifice, and sacrifice does not sell well—especially to people like us who are reaping the short-term gain without having to live the horror of the long-term damage.

Our children and grandchildren are not likely to look back and think that what we did to their air, water, and land was wonderful.

What to do? Each of us has to take personal responsibility. There is no "other" to answer for us. Government cannot solve this problem; groups cannot solve this problem. The only solution is individual responsibility, which brings individual change. The whole world is waiting for someone else to create an easy solution. An easy solution will never—I repeat, NEVER—appear. The day that we can say "Oh, good, I don't have to worry about the mess I have personally created" will never come. My goal in writing this book was to outline a way that each of us can grow more of our own food, take more personal responsibility, and do better, one house at a time. We can do it. My garden proves it can be done. Pollution and self-indulgence will never create global peace. Natural abundance is the only answer. Our children and grandchildren deserve a chance at peace.

Q: How does the no-till method make a larger garden possible?

A: As my garden has become easier and easier to manage over time, as I have created better garden designs, my garden has expanded. Today, of course, my garden has dramatically expanded as I work to save the rarest seeds on earth. But our main garden goal continues to be the same as always—to feed ourselves from the garden as much as possible with fresh, nutritious, chemical-free food. When gardening is easier, we do more of it, plain and simple. I would die a happy man if the world was filled with gardens because this book showed people how easy growing backyard food can be.

Q: Can this method be applied to large farms?

A: Yes. I recognize that not everyone can raise their own food self-reliantly. We can farm food in a smarter, more natural, more sustainable way—at prices that people can afford. I will never, never accept the answer that the world is doomed to chemicals, pollution, and unfair labor practices as our only option. I should be the busiest person in the world, in demand around the globe, helping the world change the way we farm our food. If you think I'm bluffing, or pretending, or selling snake oil, put me to the test. Wouldn't it be great if every industrial-sized farm had a "board of directors" made up of people whose only goal was to feed the world without harming the world? One day, I'm going to write a whole book on Do No Harm Gardening and Farming. Do No Harm is the only true option for feeding the world!

Raised beds waiting to be planted in the author's spring garden

ORGANIC GARDENING MADE PRACTICAL AND SIMPLE

O rganic matter is necessary for mycelium growth and sustainment. The more organic matter in your soil for the mycelium to "eat," the more mycelium there will be and the happier your soil will be. Here is a great quote about no-till gardening from Penn State Extension, which just goes to prove that if we work hand-in-hand with Mother Nature instead of fighting her every step of the way, our gardens will be healthier and easier:

> Growing crops that leave substantial amounts of residue [dead leaves, etc.] can increase soil organic matter, depending upon tillage. Crops requiring annual tillage that incorporates any residue will briefly boost organic matter content, but ultimately such tillage hastens organic matter decomposition and disappearance. A study in Delaware reported

no increase in humus over time in reduced tillage (chisel-plowed) fields while showing an almost 50 percent increase in humus for fields in no-tillage for seven or eight years. Residue left in no-till situations year after year allows for a long-term increase in soil organic matter.[1]

Once your garden is no-till, self-seeding, and not reliant on petrochemical fertilizer, it is easy to be organic. Weeds, bugs, and diseases are naturally controlled. We are now working hand-in-hand with Mother Nature, not against her. Suddenly, we have an honest, sustainable, permacultured, no-till solution that makes gardening simpler and easier for everyone.

NOTES

1. Donald R. Daum, "Soil Compaction and Conservation Tillage," Penn State Extension College of Agricultural Sciences Conservation Tillage Series, http://extension.psu.edu/plants/crops/soil-management/conservation-tillage/soil-compaction-and-conservation-tillage.

REFERENCES

Alexander, William. *The $64 Tomato: How One Man Nearly Lost His Sanity, Spent a Fortune, and Endured an Existential Crisis in the Quest for the Perfect Garden.* Chapel Hill, NC: Algonquin Books, 2006.

Back to Eden. Directed and produced by Dana Richardson and Sarah Zentz. Big Sur, CA: Dana and Sarah Films, 2011. DVD.

Daum, Donald R. "Soil Compaction and Conservation Tillage." Penn State Extension College of Agricultural Sciences Conservation Tillage Series. http://extension.psu.edu/plants/crops/soil-management/conservation-tillage/soil-compaction-and-conservation-tillage.

Escudero, Viviana, and Rodolfo Mendoza. "Seasonal variation of arbuscular mycorrhizal fungi in temperate grasslands along a wide hydrologic gradient." *Mycorrhiza* 15, no. 4 (2005): 291–9. doi: 10.1007/s00572-004-0332-3.

Finlay, Roger D. "Ecological aspects of mycorrhizal symbiosis: with special emphasis on the functional diversity of interactions involving the extraradical mycelium data." *Journal of Experimental Botany* 59, no. 5 (2008): 1115–26. http://jxb.oxfordjournals.org/content/59/5/1115.full.pdf.

Fleming, Nic. "The Largest Living Thing on Earth Is a Humongous Fungus." BBC Earth, November 19, 2014. http://www.bbc.com/earth/story/20141114-the-biggest-organism-in-the-world.

Frank, A. B. "On the nutritional dependence of certain trees on root symbiosis with belowground fungi (an English translation of A. B. Frank's classic 1885 paper)." Translated by James M. Trappe. Mycorrhiza 15 (2005): 267–75. http://bit.ly/1WYskTj

"Fukuoka, Masanobu." Ramon Magsaysay Award Foundation Website. http://www.rmaf.org.ph/newrmaf/main/awardees/awardee/profile/292.

Fukuoka, Masanobu. *The One-Straw Revolution: An Introduction to Natural Farming*. New York: NYRB Classics, 2009.

Fukuoka, Masanobu. *The Ultimatum of GOD NATURE: The One-Straw Revolution, A Recapitulation*. Trans. Shou Shin Sha. Oohira, Ehimeken, Japan: 1996.

Harthorne, Michael. "Mushrooms Make It Rain." Newser. http://www.newser.com/story/215247/mushrooms-make-it-rain.html

Hassett, Maribeth O., Mark W. F. Fischer, and Nicholas P. Money. "Mushrooms as Rainmakers: How Spores Act as Nuclei for Raindrops." PLOS One. http://journals.plos.org/plosone/article?id=10.1371/journal.pone.0140407 Redecker, Dirk, Robin Kodner, and Linda E. Graham. "Glomalean Fungi from the Ordovician." *Science* 15, Vol. 289, no. 5486 (2000): 1920–21. doi:10.1126/science.289.5486.1920.

Robbins, William J., and Harold W. Rickett. *Botany: A Textbook for College and University Students*. New York: D. Van Nostrand Company, 1929.

Stamets, Paul. *Mycelium Running: How Mushrooms Can Help Save the World*. Berkeley, CA: Ten Speed Press, 2005.

Viegas, Jennifer. "Mushrooms Promote Downpours." Discovery News. http://news.discovery.com/earth/mushrooms-promote-downpours-151028.htm#mkcpgn=rssnws1

Warnock, Caleb. *Backyard Winter Gardening: Vegetables Fresh and Simple, in Any Climate, without Artificial Heat or Electricity—The Way It's Been Done for 2,000 Years*. Springville, UT: Cedar Fort, Inc., 2013.

Warnock, Caleb. *The Forgotten Skills of Self-Sufficiency Used by the Mormon Pioneers*. Springville, UT: Cedar Fort, Inc., 2011.

Warnock, Caleb. *More Forgotten Skills of Self-Sufficiency.* Springville, UT: Cedar Fort Inc., 2014.

Warnock, Caleb, and Melissa Richardson. *The Art of Baking with Natural Yeast: Breads, Pancakes, Waffles, Cinnamon Rolls & Muffins.* Springville, UT: Cedar Fort, Inc., 2012.

A mushroom in Yellowstone National Park, photographed by the author

ABOUT THE AUTHOR

Caleb Warnock is the popular author of fourteen books, including *Forgotten Skills of Self-Sufficiency Used by the Mormon Pioneers, The Art of Baking with Natural Yeast, Backyard Winter Gardening For All Climates, More Forgotten Skills*, and the *Backyard Renaissance Collection*. He is the owner of SeedRenaissance.com, where you can sign up for his email newsletters. Find his Youtube channel at http://bit.ly/1OevHxT

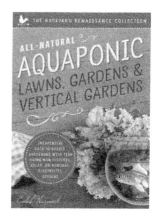

ABOUT FAMILIUS

VISIT OUR WEBSITE: www.familius.com

JOIN OUR FAMILY: There are lots of ways to connect with us! Subscribe to our newsletters at www.familius.com to receive uplifting daily inspiration, essays from our Pater Familius, a free ebook every month, and the first word on special discounts and Familius news.

GET BULK DISCOUNTS: If you feel a few friends and family might benefit from what you've read, let us know and we'll be happy to provide you with quantity discounts. Simply email us at specialorders@familius.com.

CONNECT:

www.facebook.com/paterfamilius
@familiustalk, @paterfamilius1
www.pinterest.com/familius

FAMILIUS

CPSIA information can be obtained at www.ICGtesting.com
Printed in the USA
BVOW08s0423090616

450967BV00003B/2/P

9 781942 934080